DISNEY SONGS FOR UKULELE

ARRANGED BY JIM BELOFF

T0088522

ISBN 978-1-4234-9560-4

WONDERLAND MUSIC COMPANY, INC.
WALT DISNEY MUSIC COMPANY

DISTRIBUTED BY

7777 W. BLUEMOUND RD. P.O. BOX 13819 MILWAUKEE, WI 53213

Alice in Wonderland

from Walt Disney's ALICE IN WONDERLAND
Words by Bob Hilliard
Music by Sammy Fain

Bridge
Verse
Em7 A7 Dm7 G7 C Dm7 G7
see? Where can it be? Where do
C Am Dm7 G7 C
stars go? Where is the cres - cent moon? They
B7 Em7 A7 Dm7
must be some - where in the sun - ny af - ter -
G7 Cdim7 C G7 C
noon. Al - ice in Won - der - land,
F6 G7 C F6 G7
where is the path to Won - der - land? O - ver the hill or
C D7 Dm7 G7 C
here or there? I won - der where.

Beauty and the Beast

from Walt Disney's BEAUTY AND THE BEAST
Lyrics by Howard Ashman
Music by Alan Menken

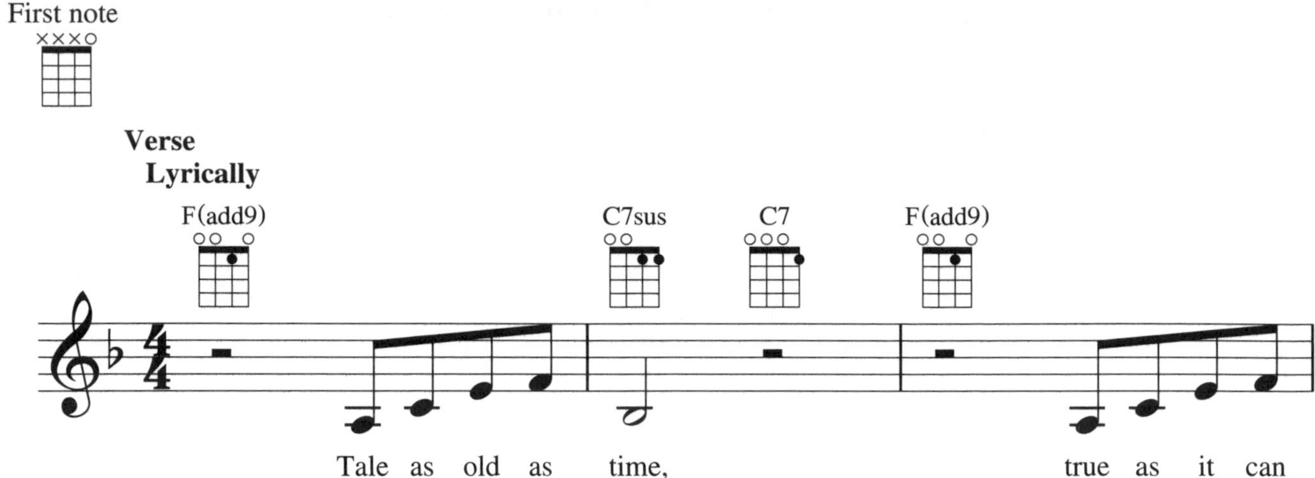

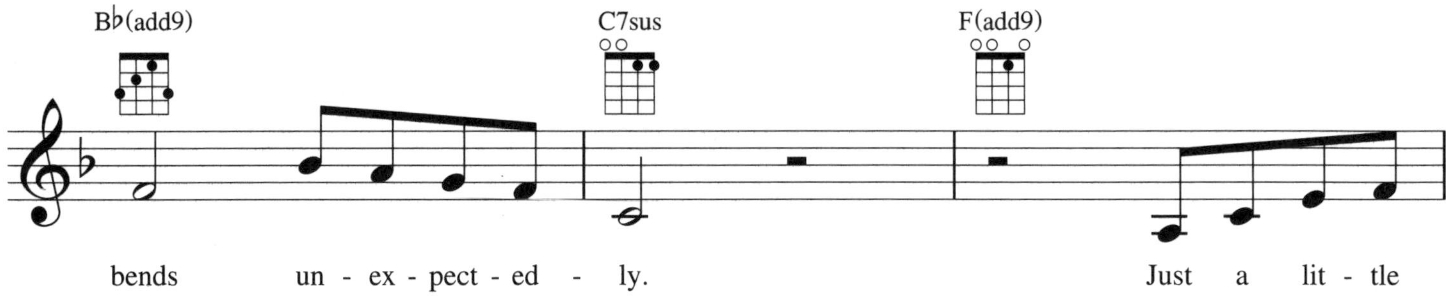

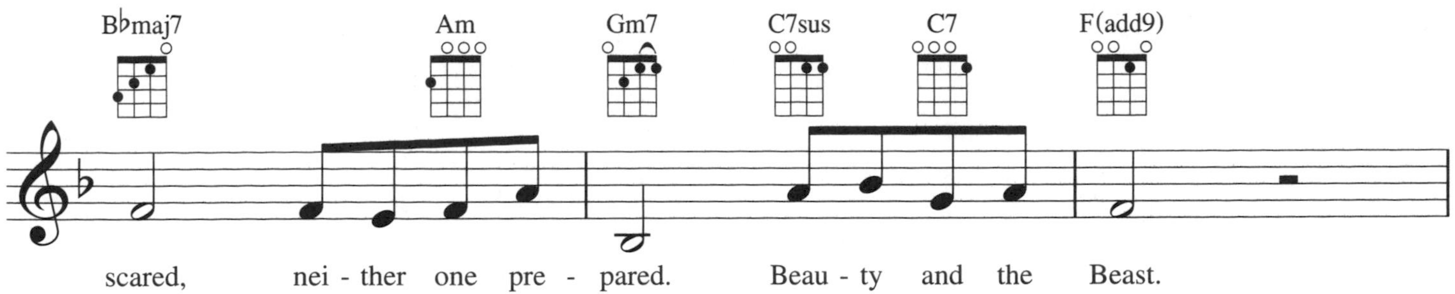
B♭maj7
Am
Gm7
C7sus
C7
F(add9)
scared, nei - ther one pre - pared. Beau - ty and the Beast.

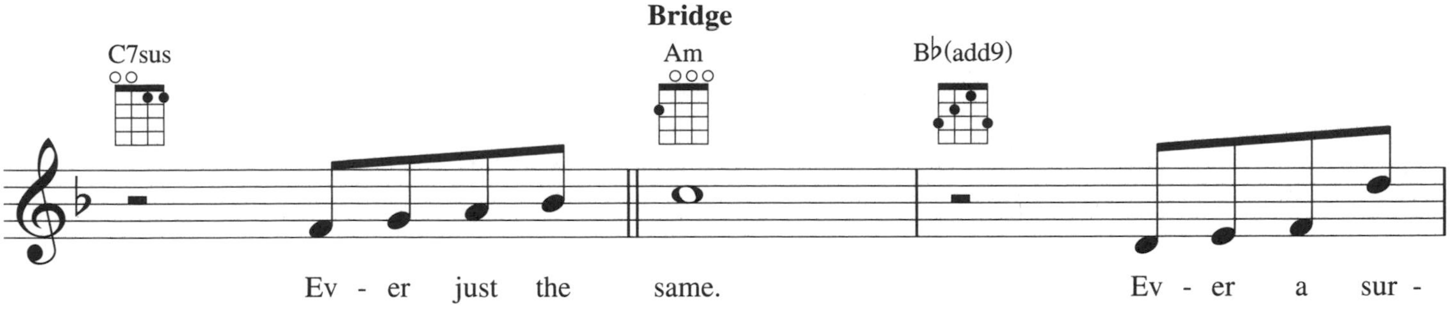
Bridge
C7sus
Am
B♭(add9)
Ev - er just the same. Ev - er a sur -

Am
B♭(add9)
Am
prise. Ev - er as be - fore, ev - er just as

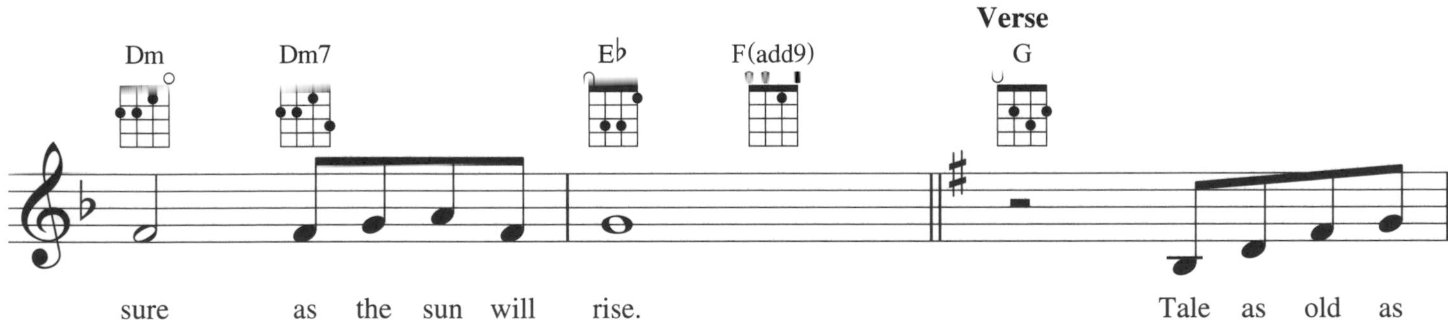
Verse
Dm
Dm7
E♭
F(add9)
G
sure as the sun will rise. Tale as old as

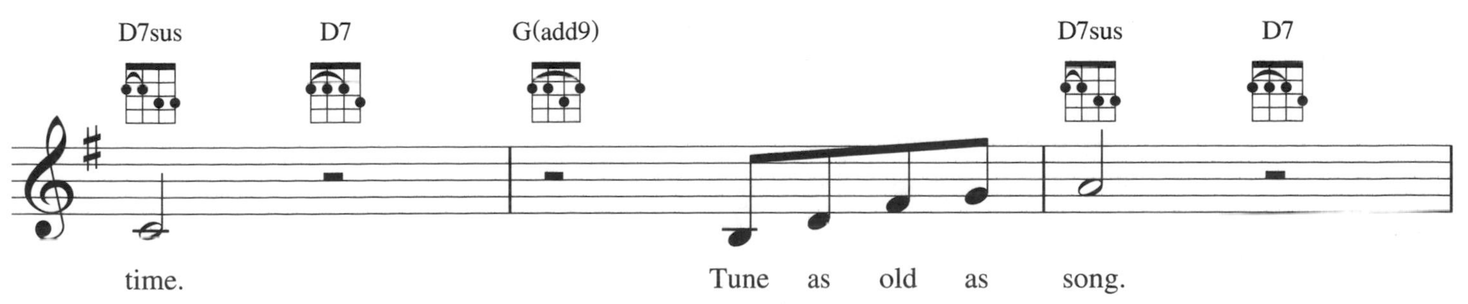
D7sus
D7
G(add9)
D7sus
D7
time. Tune as old as song.

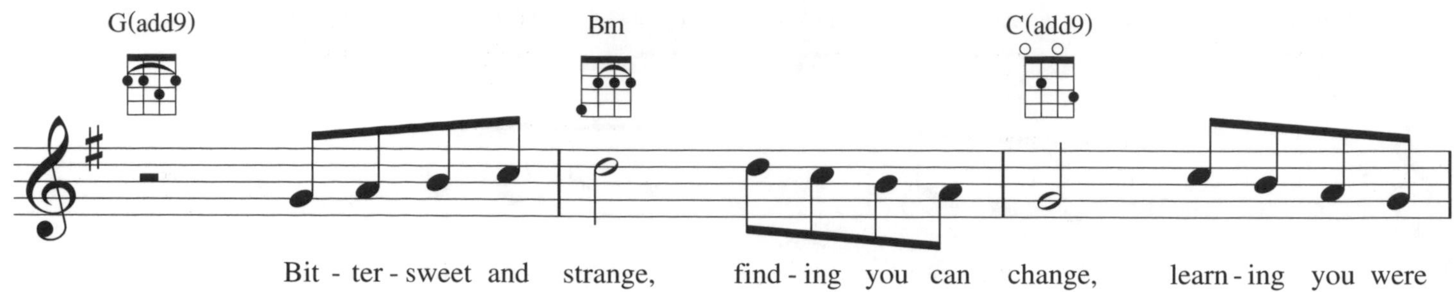
G(add9)
Bm
C(add9)
Bit - ter - sweet and strange, find - ing you can change, learn - ing you were

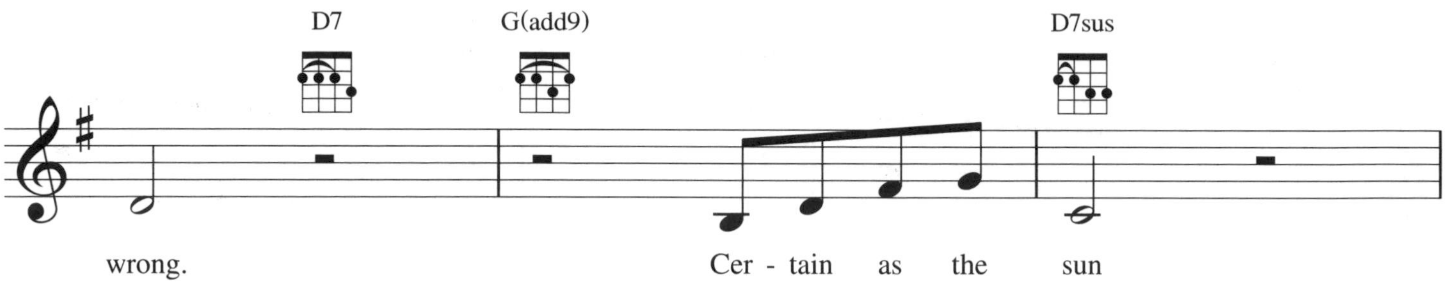
D7
G(add9)
D7sus
wrong. Cer - tain as the sun

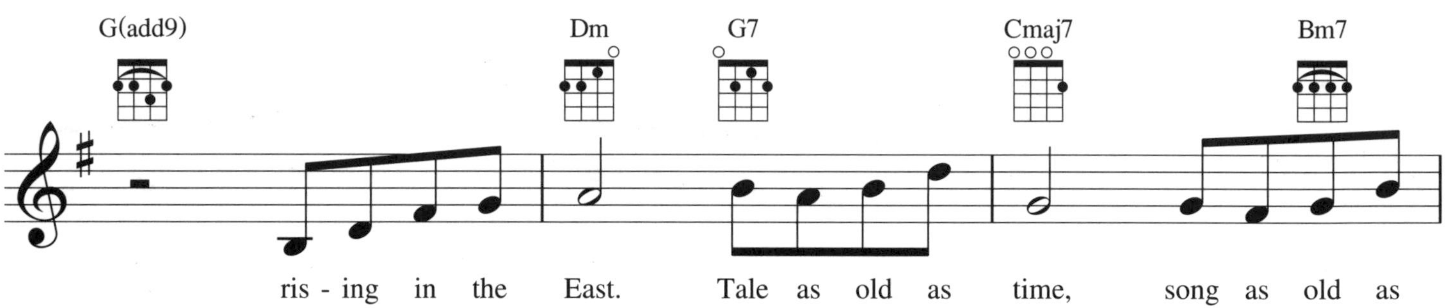
G(add9)
Dm
G7
Cmaj7
Bm7
ris - ing in the East. Tale as old as time, song as old as

Outro
Am
D7
G(add9)
Em
Bm
rhyme. Beau - ty and the Beast. Tale as old as

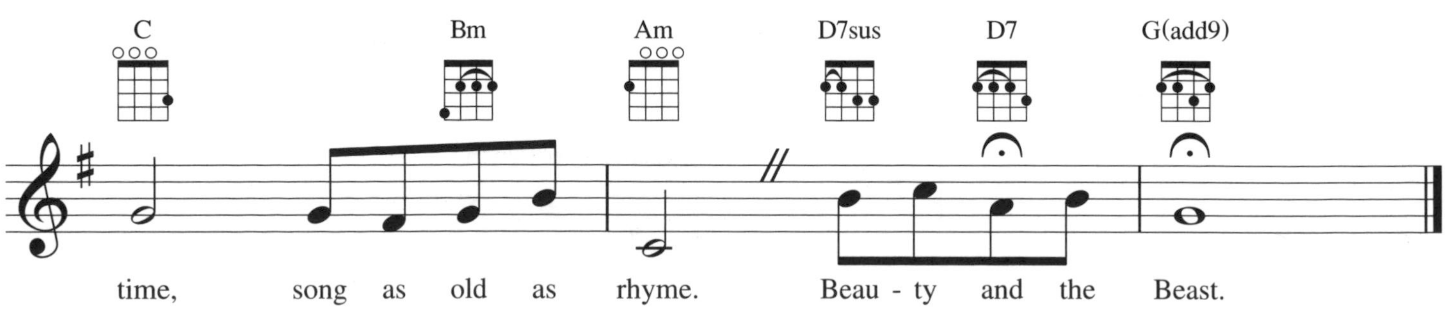
C
Bm
Am
D7sus
D7
G(add9)
time, song as old as rhyme. Beau - ty and the Beast.

Circle of Life

from Walt Disney Pictures' THE LION KING
Music by Elton John
Lyrics by Tim Rice

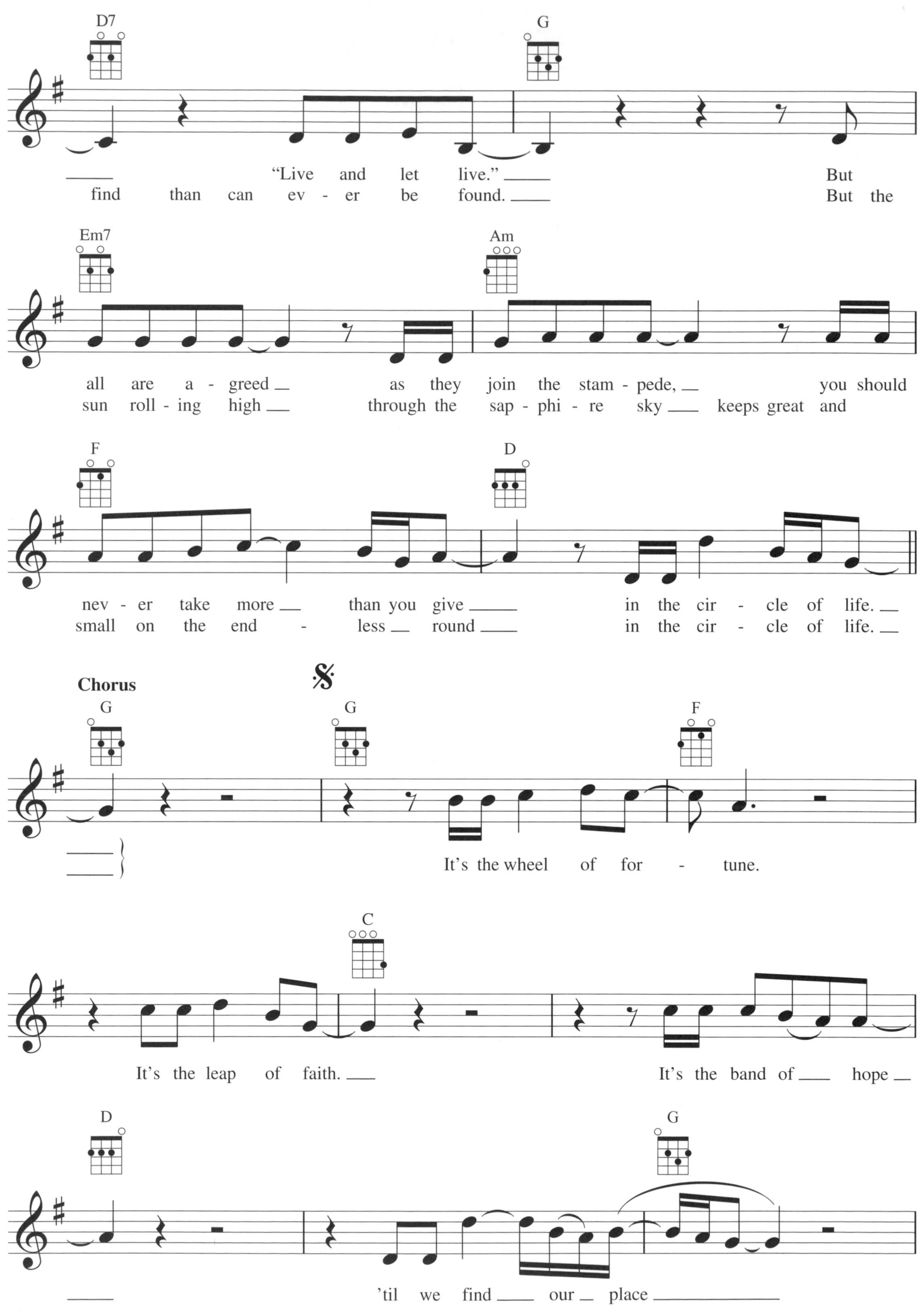
D7
G
"Live and let live."
But
find than can ev - er be found.
But the
Em7
Am
all are a - greed as they join the stam - pede, you should
sun roll - ing high through the sap - phi - re sky keeps great and
F
D
nev - er take more than you give in the cir - cle of life.
small on the end - less round in the cir - cle of life.
Chorus
G
G
F
It's the wheel of for - tune.
C
It's the leap of faith.
It's the band of hope
D
G
'til we find our place

E7
Am
E♭(add2)
on the path un - wind - ing
in the cir -
G
To Coda
1.
D
C
- cle,
the cir - cle of life.
G
2.
D
D.S. al Coda
G
C
the cir - cle of life!
Coda
D
C
G
the cir - cle of life.
Outro
E7
Am
E♭(add2)
G
On the path un - wind - ing
in the cir - cle,
Dsus
D
C
E♭
G
the cir - cle of life.

Bibbidi-Bobbidi-Boo
(The Magic Song)

from Walt Disney's CINDERELLA
Words by Jerry Livingston
Music by Mack David and Al Hoffman

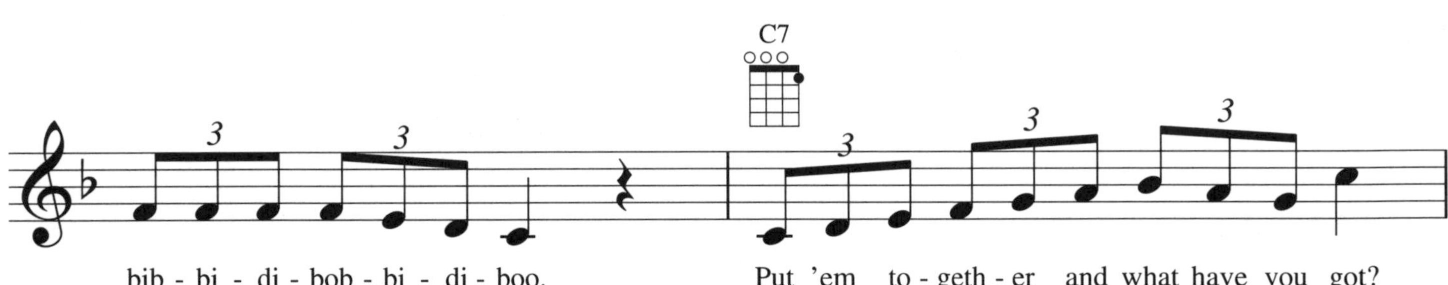

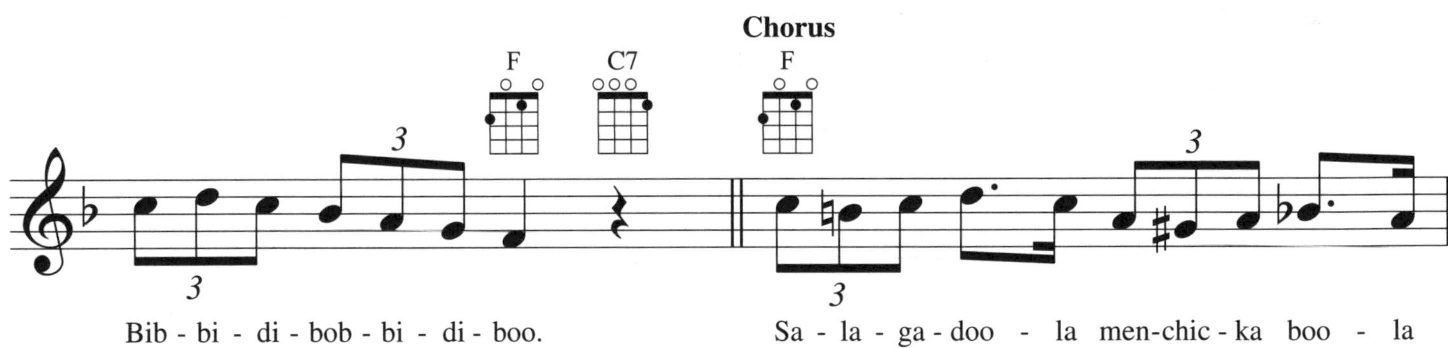

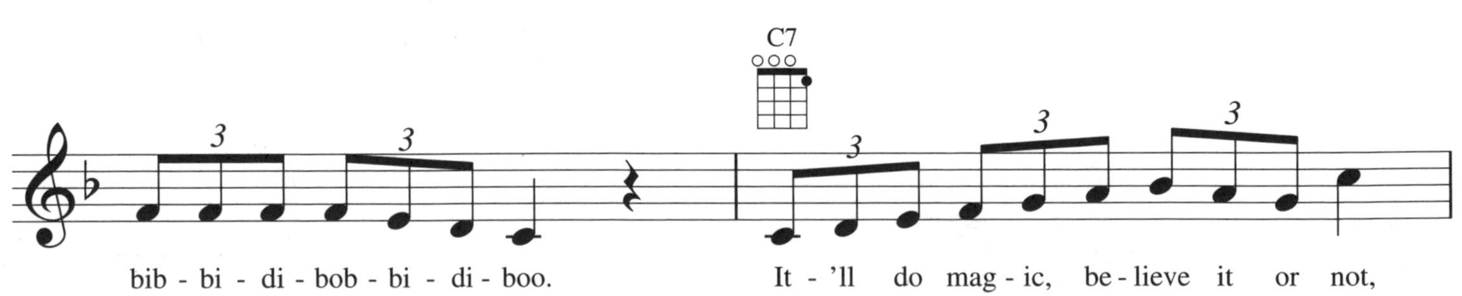

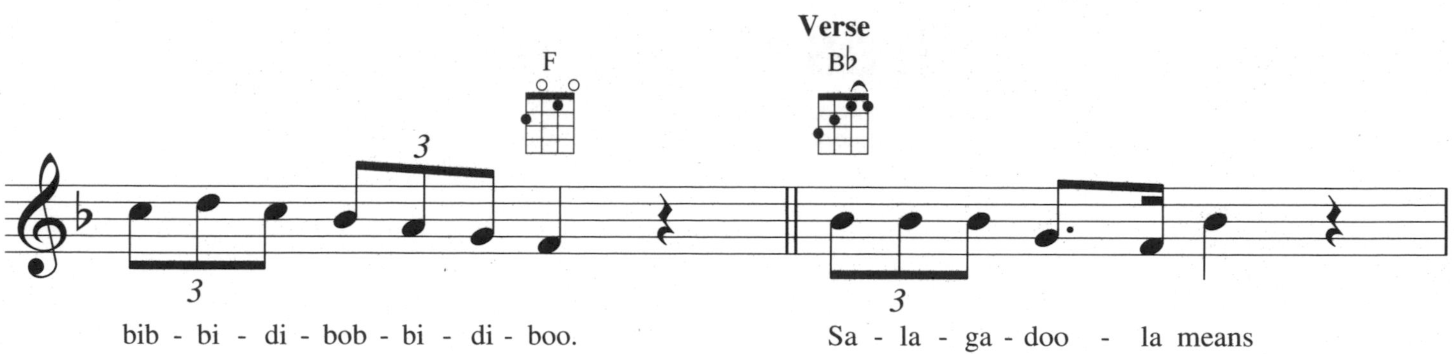
Verse
F
B♭
bib - bi - di - bob - bi - di - boo.
Sa - la - ga - doo - la means

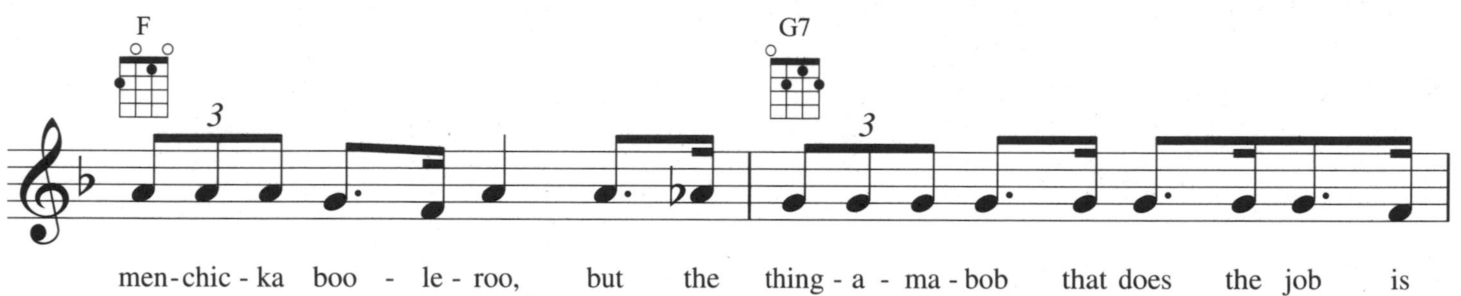
F
G7
men-chic - ka boo - le - roo, but the thing - a - ma - bob that does the job is

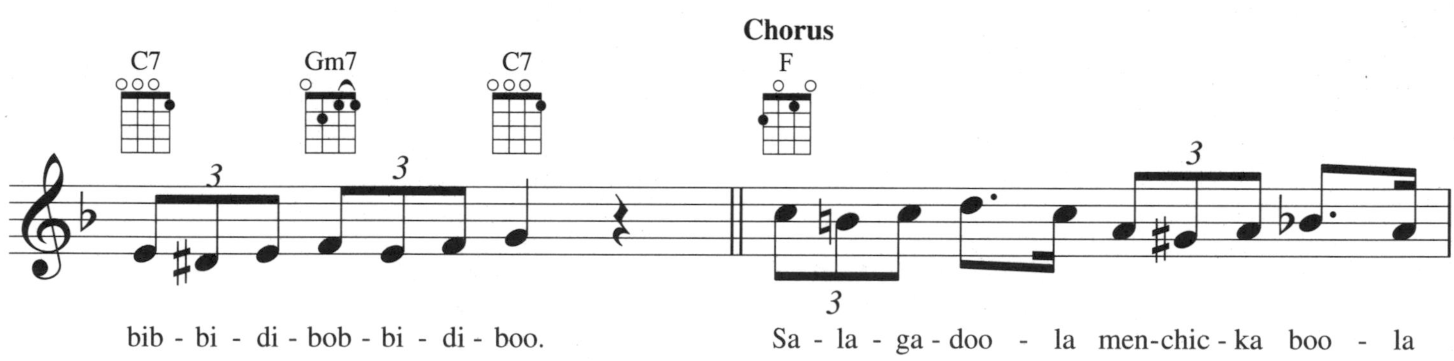
Chorus
C7
Gm7
C7
F
bib - bi - di - bob - bi - di - boo.
Sa - la - ga - doo - la men-chic - ka boo - la

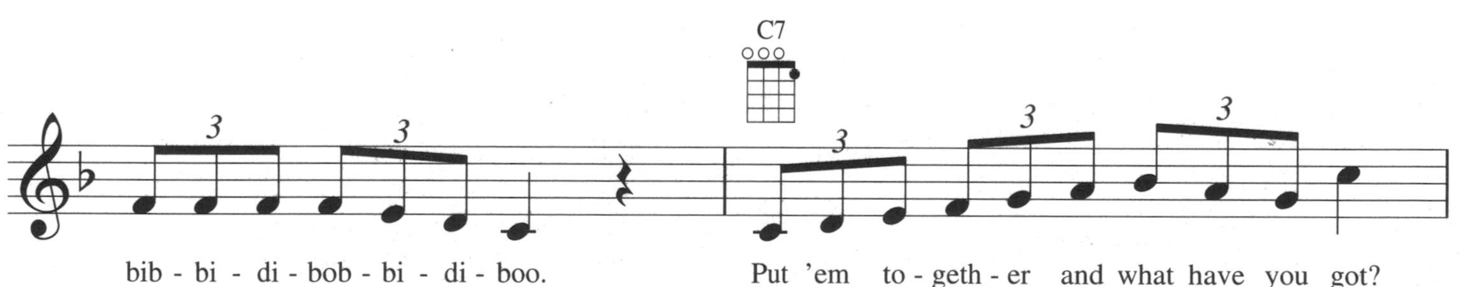
C7
bib - bi - di - bob - bi - di - boo.
Put 'em to - geth - er and what have you got?

F
Bib - bi - di - bob - bi - di, bib - bi - di - bob - bi - di, bib - bi - di - bob - bi - di - boo.

Breaking Free

from the Disney Channel Original Movie HIGH SCHOOL MUSICAL
Words and Music by Jamie Houston

Am
D
F
cre - at - ing space be - tween us, till we're sep-'rate hearts.
con-nect - ed by a feel - in', oh, in our ver - y souls,
C
G
F
D7
But your faith, it gives me strength,
ris - ing till it lifts us up so
F(add2)
Chorus
Am
strength to be - lieve.
ev - 'ry - one can see?
We're soar - in', fly -
D
F
C
G
in'. There's not a star in heav - en that we can't reach.
Am
D
F(add2)
If we're try - in', yeah, we're break - in' free. Oh, we're break-
Chorus
Am
D
in' free. Run - nin', climb - in', to

F C G Am
get to that place _ to be ___ all that we ___ can be. ___ Now's the time, _
D F(add2) C G
___ so we're break - in' free. We're break - in' free.
Bridge
F D7
More than hope, more than faith, this is truth, this is fate;
F
and to - geth - er, we see ___ it com - in'. ___
D7
Male: More than you, more than me, Female: not a want, but a need:
Chorus
F Bm
Both: both of us break - in' free. ___ Female: Soar - in', ___ Male: fly -
E(add2) G D A
- in'. ___ Both: There's not a star ___ in heav - en that we ___ can't reach. _

Bm
E
G
If we're try - in', yeah, we're break - in' free.
Bm
E
We're run - nin', ooh, climb - in' to
G
D
A
Bm
get to the place to be all that we can be. Now's the time,
E
G(add2)
Female:
so we're break - in' free.
Male:
Oh, we're break - in' free.
Outro-Verse
Bm
E
G(add2)
You know the world can see us in a way that's
rit.
D
A
Gmaj7
dif - f'rent from who we are.

Can You Feel the Love Tonight

from Walt Disney Pictures' THE LION KING
Music by Elton John
Lyrics by Tim Rice

G
C
A7
D
It is where we are.
how it's laid to rest?
C
G
Em
C
It's e - nough for this wide - eyed wan - der - er
It's e - nough to make kings and vag - a - bonds be -
To Coda
1., 3.
2.
Am
G
C
A7
D
C
that we got this far. And
lieve the ver - y best.
D.C. al Coda
(with repeat)
Coda
G
C
G
ver - y best.
C
G
Em
C
It's e - nough to make kings and vag - a - bonds be -
Am
G
C
G
lieve the ver - y best.

Chim Chim Cher-ee

from Walt Disney's MARY POPPINS

Words and Music by Richard M. Sherman and Robert B. Sherman

Verse
Am
E+
Am7
D
Now, as the lad - der of life 'as been strung, you
I choose me bris - tles with pride, yes, I do: a
(D.S.) Up where the smoke is all bill - ered and curled, 'tween
Dm
Am
B7
may think a sweep's on the bot - tom - most
broom for the shaft and a brush for the
pave - ment and star is the chim - ney sweep
E7
Am
E+
rung. Though I spends me time in the
flue. Though I'm cov - ered with soot from me
world. When there's 'ard - ly no day nor
Am7
D
Dm
ash - es and smoke, in this 'ole wide
'ead to me toes, a sweep knows 'e's
'ard - ly no night, there's things 'alf in
To Coda
1.
2. D.S. al Coda
Am
E7
Am
Am
world there's no 'ap - pi - er bloke.
wel - come wher - ev - er 'e goes.
shad - ow and 'alf - way in

Coda
Am
Dm
Am
E7
light. On the roof - tops of Lon - don, coo, what a
Chorus
Am
Am
E+
Am7
sight! Chim chim - in - ey, chim chim - in - ey, chim chim cher -
D
Dm
Am
B7
E7
ee! When you're with a sweep you're in glad com - pa - ny.
Am
E+
Am7
D
No - where is there a more 'ap - pi - er crew than
Dm
Am
E7
Am
them wot sings, "Chim chim cher - ee, chim cher - oo!"
Dm
Am
E7
Am
Chim chim - in - ey, chim chim, cher - ee, chim cher - oo!

Heigh-Ho

The Dwarfs' Marching Song from Walt Disney's SNOW WHITE AND THE SEVEN DWARFS
Words by Larry Morey
Music by Frank Churchill

A Dream Is a Wish Your Heart Makes

from Walt Disney's CINDERELLA

Words and Music by Mack David, Al Hoffman and Jerry Livingston

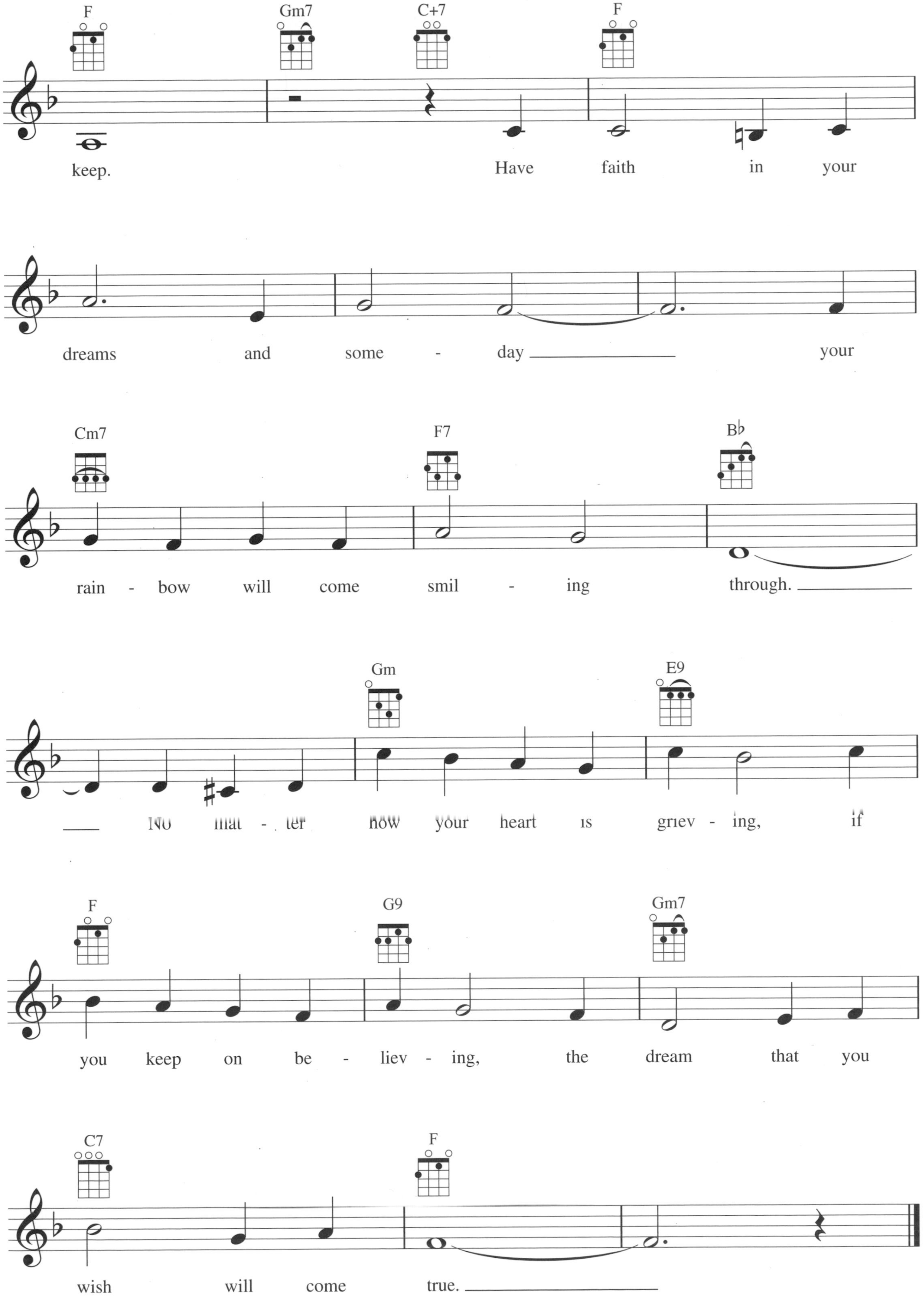

F Gm7 C+7 F

keep. Have faith in your

dreams and some - day ___ your

Cm7 F7 B♭

rain - bow will come smil - ing through. ___

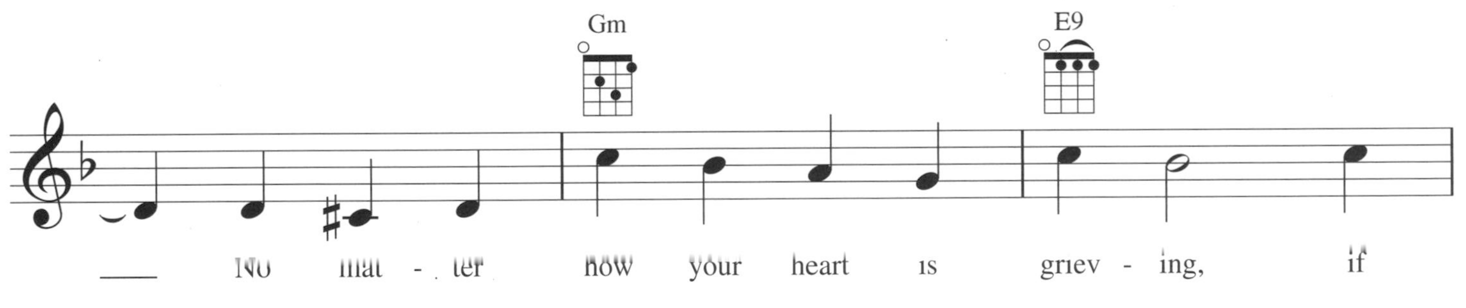

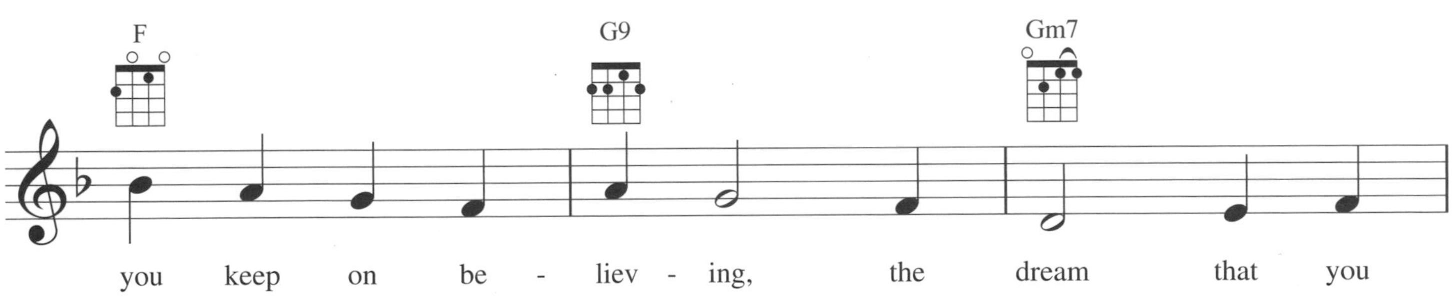

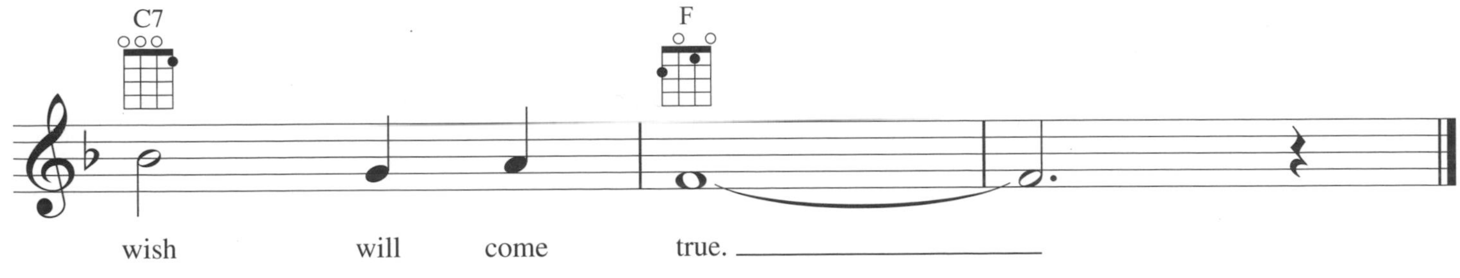

Give a Little Whistle

from Walt Disney's PINOCCHIO
Words by Ned Washington
Music by Leigh Harline

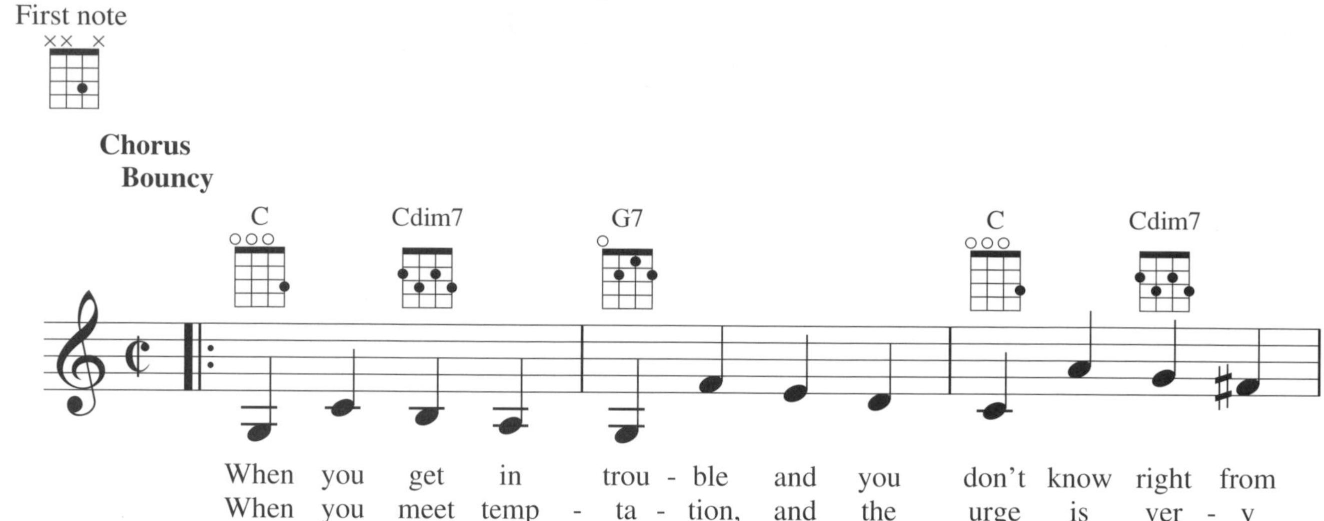

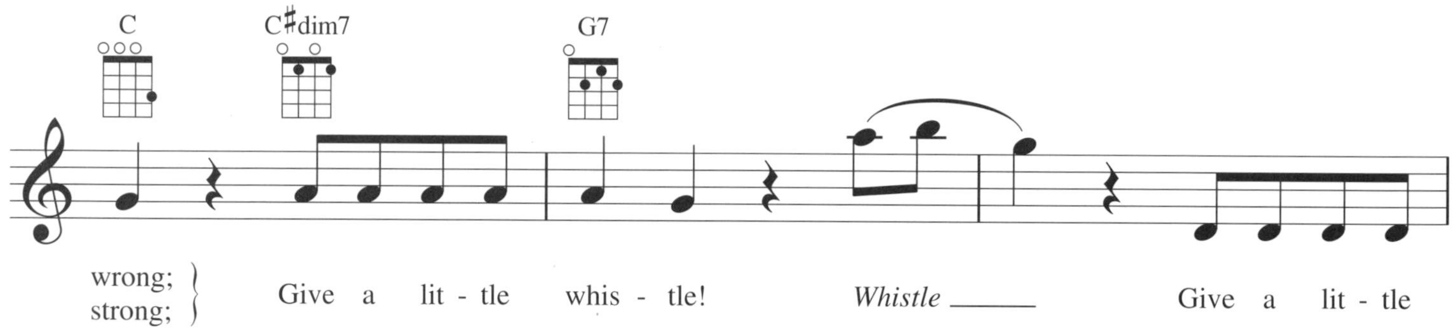

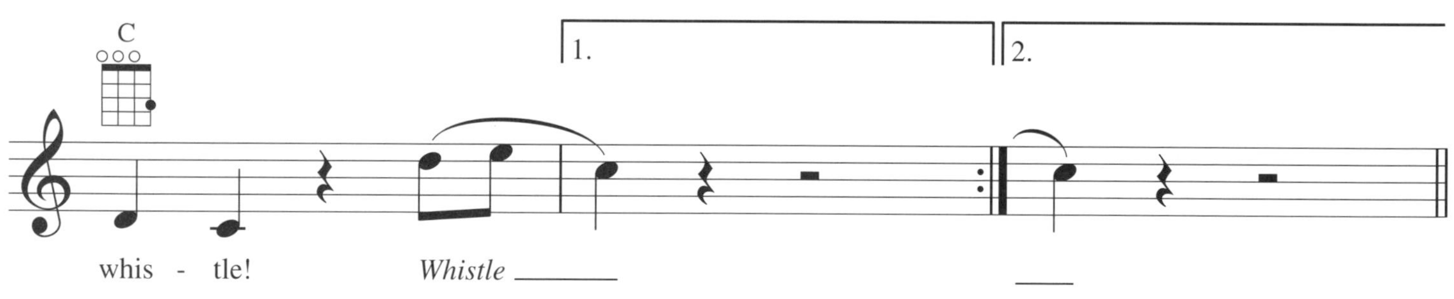

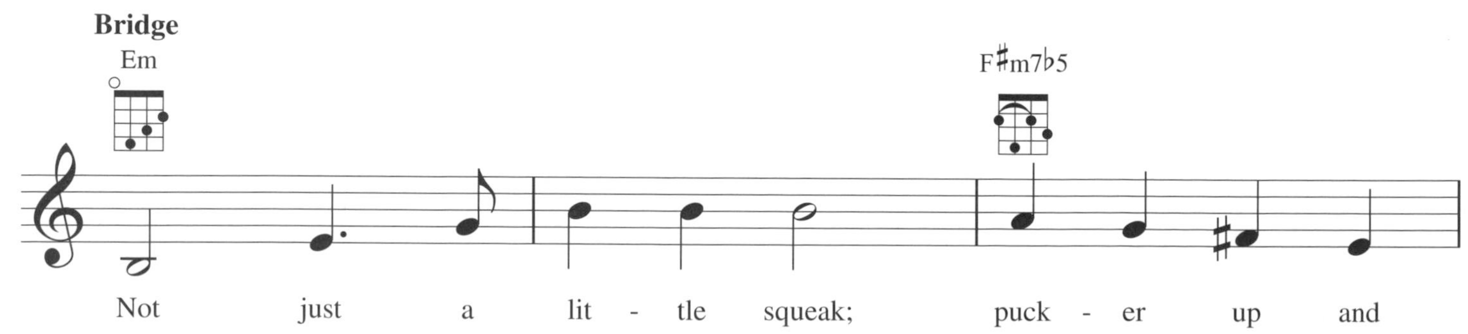

B
B7
blow. And if your whis - tle's weak;
Chorus
Em
D♯dim7
G7
C
Cdim7
yell, "Jim - i - ny Crick - et." Take the straight and
G7
C
Cdim7
C
C♯dim7
nar - row path and if you start to slide; Give a lit - tle
G7
D♯dim7
whis - tle! Whistle ______ Give a lit - tle
A7
Dm7
whis - tle! Whistle ______ And al - ways let your
G7
C
G7
C
con - science be your guide.

It's a Small World

from Disneyland Resort® and Magic Kingdom® Park
Words and Music by Richard M. Sherman and Robert B. Sherman

Chorus
G
all.
all.
It's a
D7
small world af - ter all,
G
it's a small world af - ter
G7
all. It's a small world
C
Am
D7
af - ter all. It's a small,
G
1.
2.
small world. There is

Mickey Mouse March

from Walt Disney's THE MICKEY MOUSE CLUB

Words and Music by Jimmie Dodd

Supercalifragilisticexpialidocious

from Walt Disney's MARY POPPINS
Words and Music by Richard M. Sherman and Robert B. Sherman

Interlude
C
G7
C
Um did - dle did - dle did - dle, um did - dle ay! Um did - dle did - dle did - dle,
G7
Verse
C
um did - dle ay!
Be - cause I was a - fraid to speak when
He trav - eled all a - round the world and
So when the cat has got your tongue, there's
C♯dim7
G7
I was just a lad, me fa - ther gave me
ev - 'ry - where he went he'd use his word and
no need for dis - may. Just sum - mon up this
C
nose a tweak and told me I was bad. But
all would say, "There goes a clev - er gent!" When
word and then you've got a lot to say. But
C7
then one day I learned a word that saved me ach - in'
dukes and ma - 'a - ra - jas pass the time of day with
bet - ter use it care - ful - ly or it can change your
F
D7
nose, the big - gest word you ev - er 'eard and
me, I say me spe - cial word and then they
life. One night I said it to me girl and

Chorus
G7
C
this is 'ow it goes: Oh!
ask me out to tea. Oh!
now me girl's me wife. She's
(1.,2.) Su - per - cal - i -
(3.) Su - per - cal - i -
C♯dim7
G7
frag - il - is - tic - ex - pi - al - i - do - cious!
frag - il - is - tic - ex - pi - al - i - do - cious!
E - ven though the sound of it is some - thing quite a -
Su - per - cal - i - frag - il - is - tic - ex - pi - al - i -
C
tro - cious, if you say it loud e - nough, you'll
do - cious! Su - per - cal - i - frag - il - is - tic -
C7
F
al - ways sound pre - co - cious. Su - per - cal - i -
ex - pi - al - i - do - cious! Su - per - cal - i -
1., 2.
3.
C
G7
C
C
frag - il - is - tic - ex - pi - al - i - do - cious!
frag - il - is - tic - ex - pi - al - i - do - cious!

Some Day My Prince Will Come

from Walt Disney's SNOW WHITE AND THE SEVEN DWARFS

Words by Larry Morey
Music by Frank Churchill

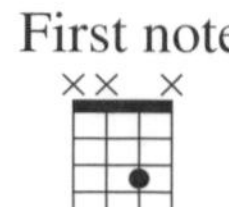

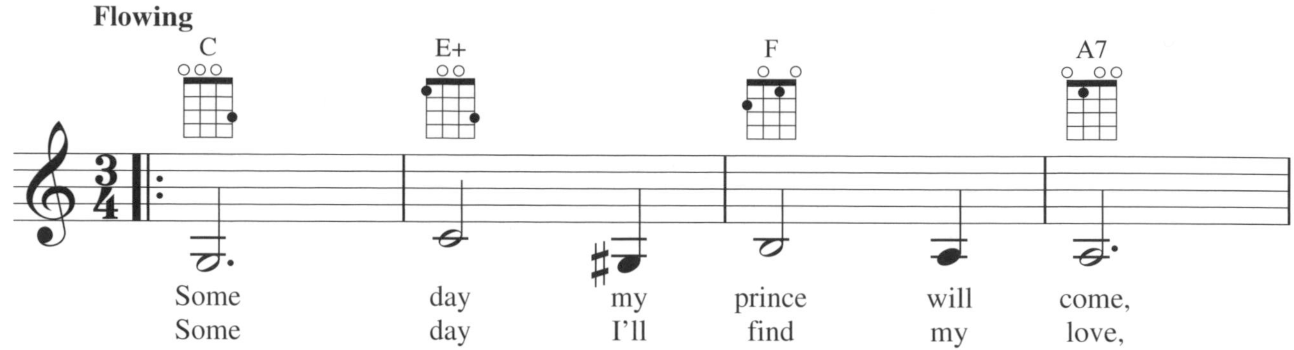

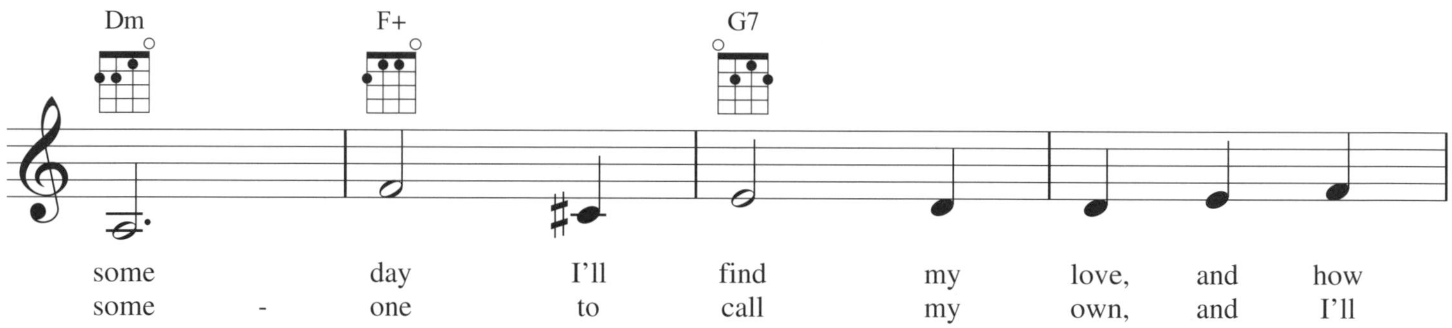

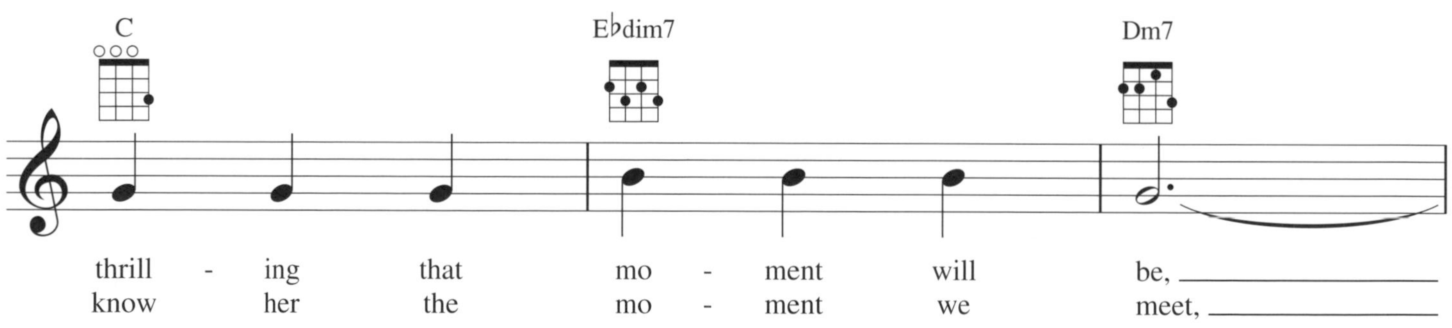

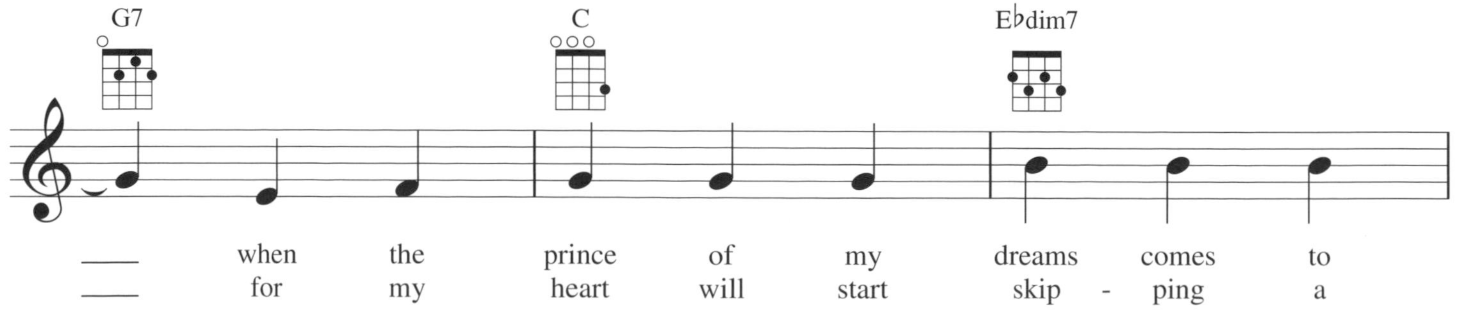

Dm7
G7
C
E+
me.
beat.
He'll whis - per
Some day we'll
F
A7
Dm
F+
"I love you" And steal a
say and do things we've been
G7
C
E7
E+
kiss or two. Though he's
long - ing to. Though she's
far a - way, I'll
C
Edim7
Dm7
G7
find my love some day, some day when my dreams come
1.
2.
C
Dm7
G7
C
true.
true.

When You Wish Upon a Star

from Walt Disney's PINOCCHIO
Words by Ned Washington
Music by Leigh Harline

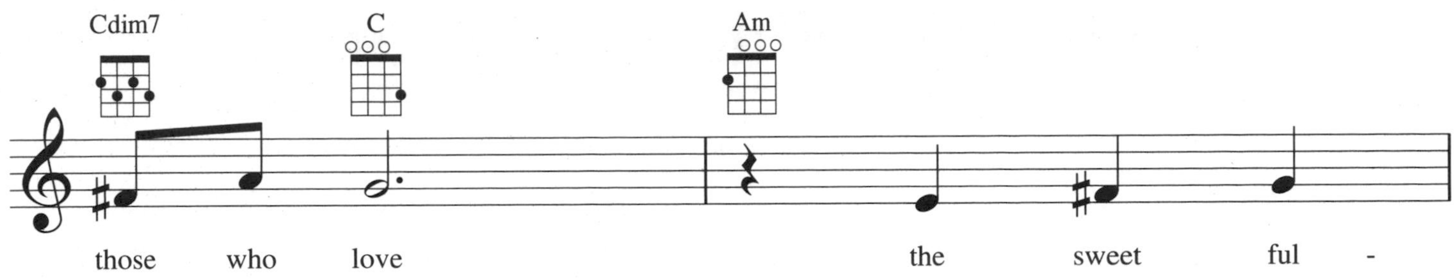
Cdim7
C
Am
those who love the sweet ful -

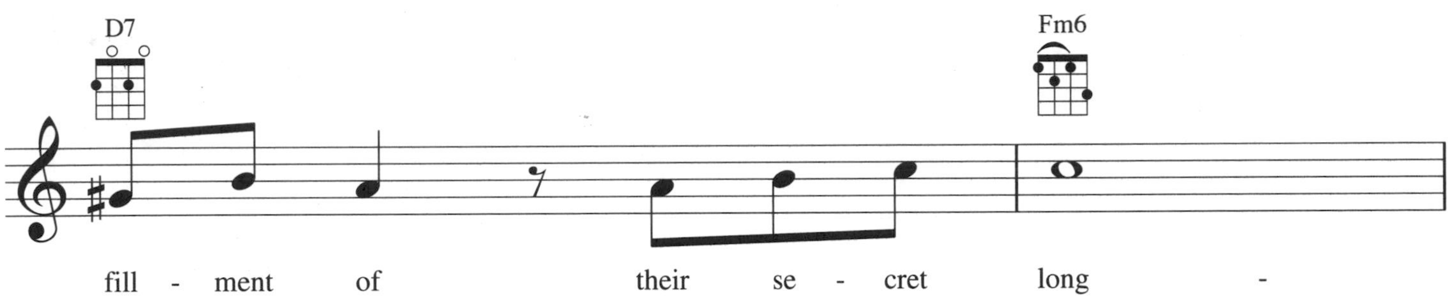
D7
Fm6
fill - ment of their se - cret long -

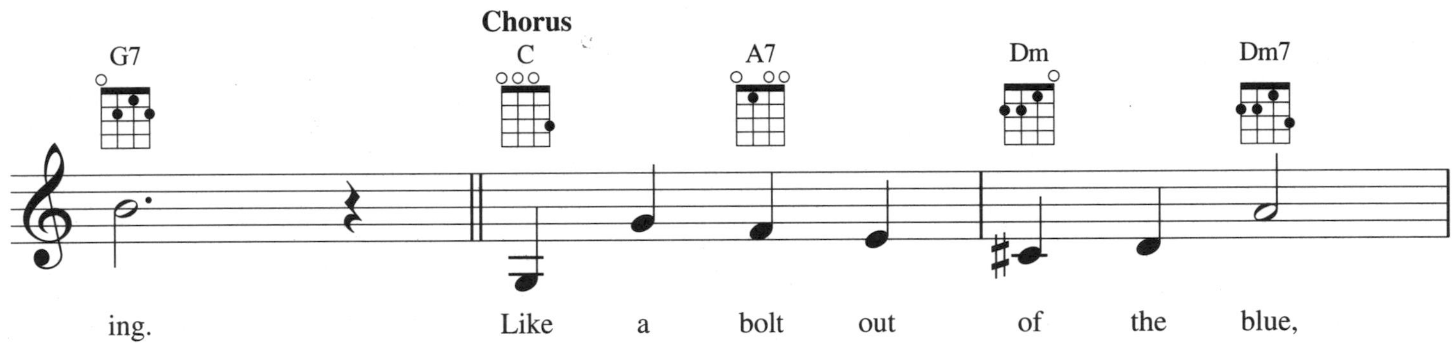
Chorus
G7
C
A7
Dm
Dm7
ing. Like a bolt out of the blue,

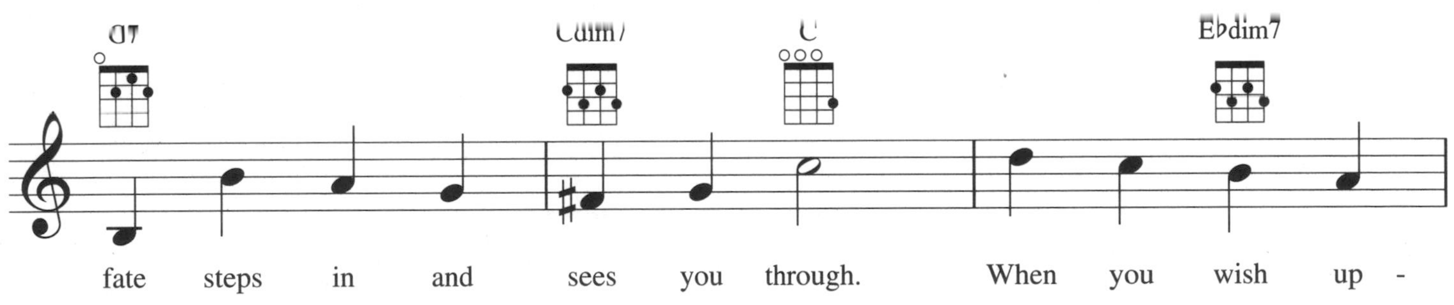
E♭dim7
fate steps in and sees you through. When you wish up -

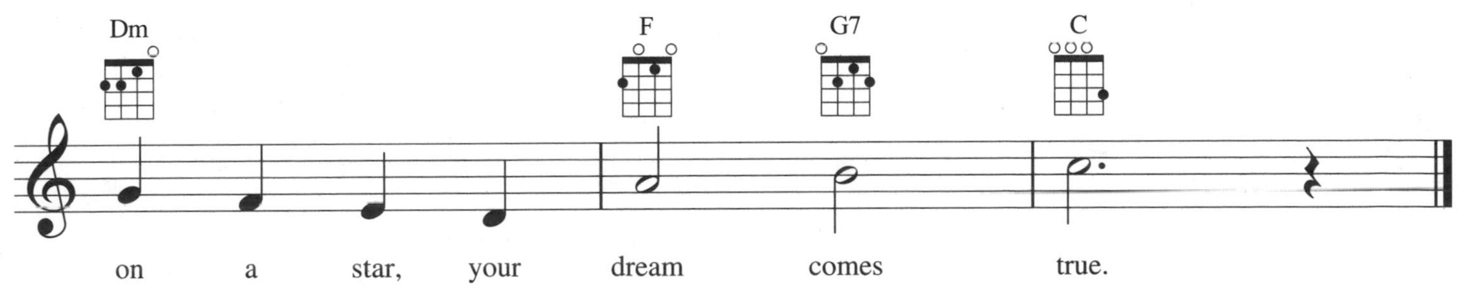
Dm
F
G7
C
on a star, your dream comes true.

Whistle While You Work

from Walt Disney's SNOW WHITE AND THE SEVEN DWARFS
Words by Larry Morey
Music by Frank Churchill

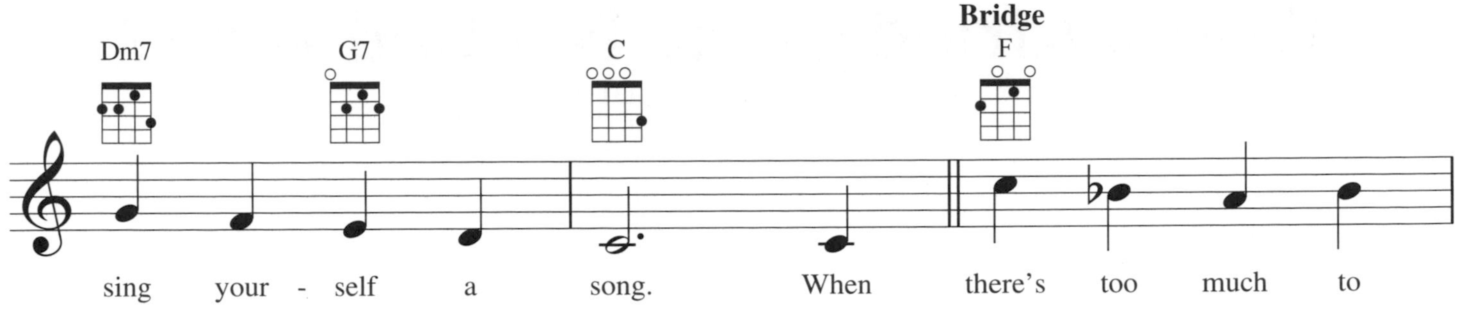
Bridge
Dm7
G7
C
F
sing your - self a song. When there's too much to

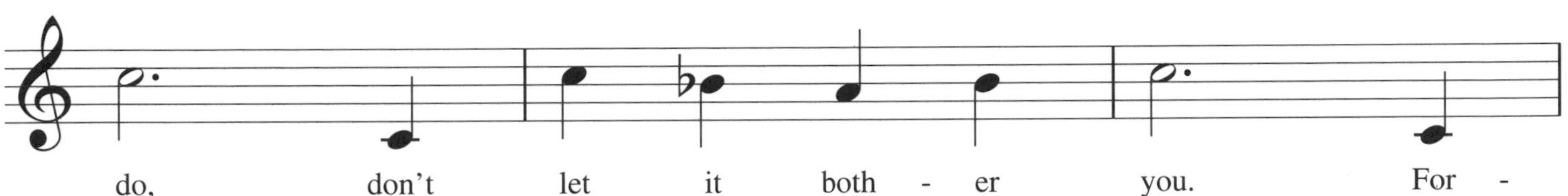
do, don't let it both - er you. For -

Fm
C
C♯dim7
get your trou - ble, try to be just like the cheer - ful

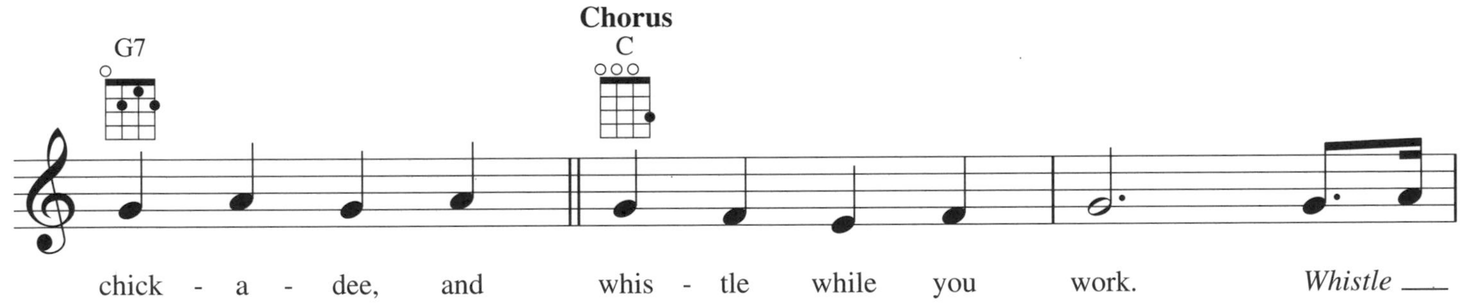
Chorus
G7
C
chick - a - dee, and whis - tle while you work. *Whistle*

Dm7
G7
Come on, get smart, tune

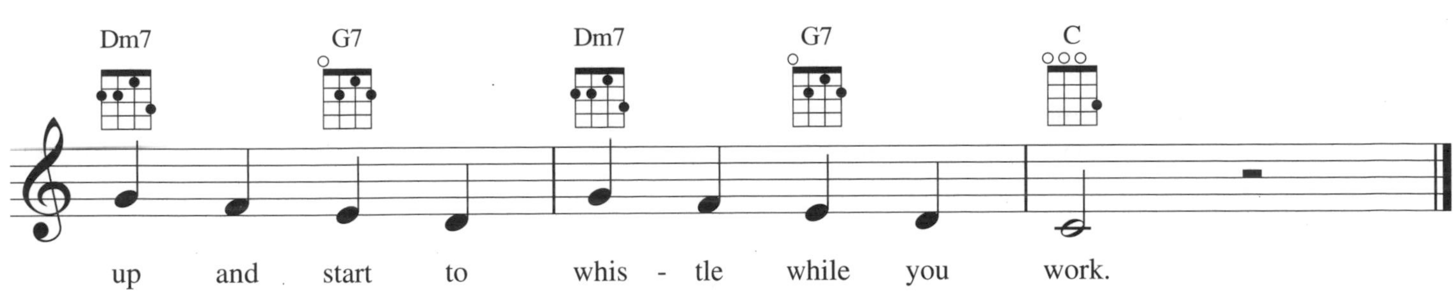
Dm7
G7
Dm7
G7
C
up and start to whis - tle while you work.

Who's Afraid of the Big Bad Wolf?

from Walt Disney's THREE LITTLE PIGS
Words and Music by Frank Churchill
Additional Lyric by Ann Ronell

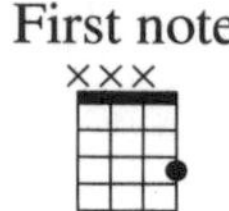

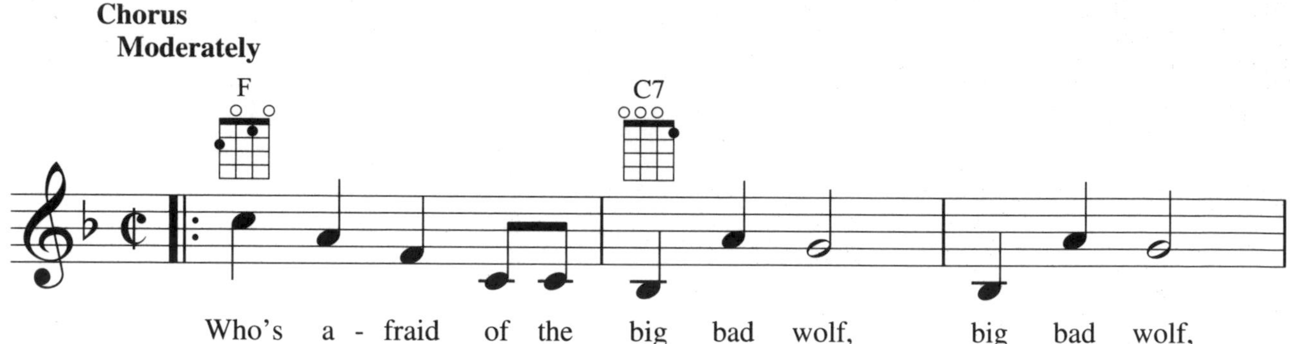

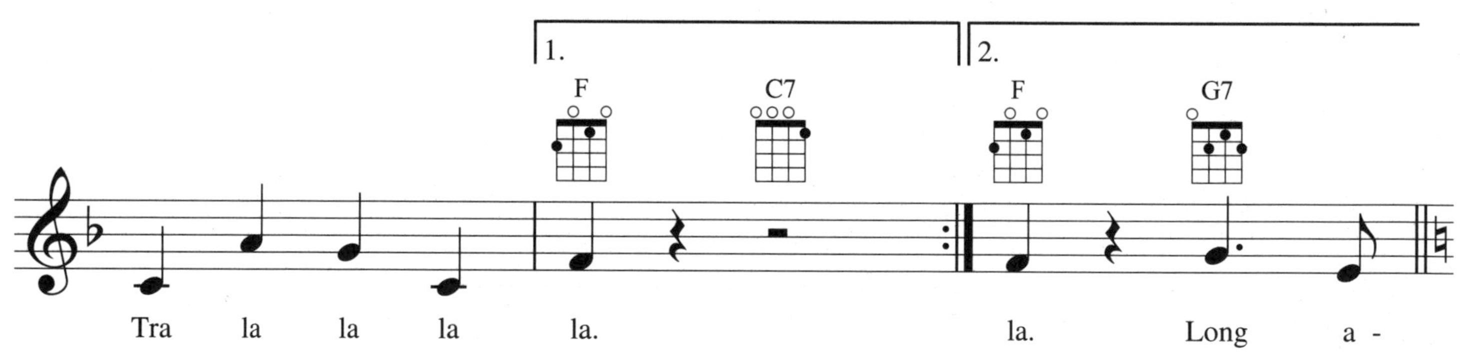

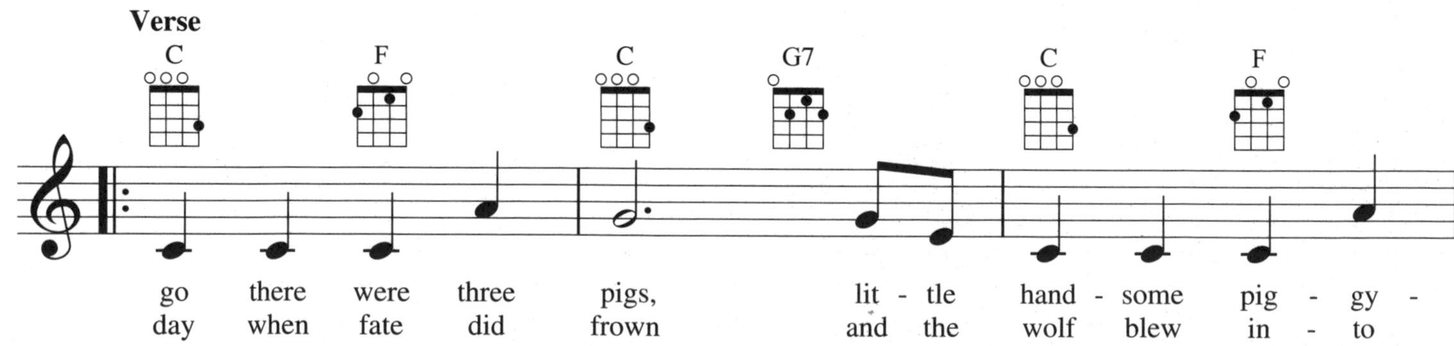

C
G7
C
F
C
wigs. For the big bad, ver - y big, ver - y bad wolf they
town. With a gruff "puff, puff" he puffed just e - nough, and the
G7
C
G7
C
F
did - n't give three figs. Num - ber one was ver - y
hay house fell right down. One and two were scared to
C
G7
C
F
C
G7
gay, and he built his house with hay. With a
death of the big bad wolf - ie's breath. "By the
C
F
C
G7
hey - hey toot he blew on his flute, and he played a - round all
hair of your chin - ny - chin I'll blow you in." And the twig house an - swered
C
C7
F
B7
Em
A7
day. Num - ber two was fond of jigs, and
yes. No one left but num - ber three to

Dm G7 C F B7
so he built his house with twigs. Heigh did-dle did - dle, he
save the pig - let fam - i - ly. When they _ knocked _ he
Em A7 D7 G G7
played on his fid - dle and danced with la - dy pigs. Num - ber
fast un - locked _ and said, "Come in with me!" Now they
C F C G7 C F
three said, "Nix on tricks. I will build my house with
all were safe in - side, and the bricks hurt wolf - ie's
C G7 C F C
bricks." He had no chance to sing and _ dance 'cause _
pride. So he slid down the chim - ney and, oh, by ___ Jim - 'ney, in the
G7 C
Pre-Chorus
N.C.
work and play don't mix! Ha - ha - ha! The
fi - re he was fried! Ha - ha - ha! The
two lit - tle, do lit - tle pigs just winked and
three lit - tle, free lit - tle pigs re - joiced and

Chorus
F
C7
laughed ha - ha!
laughed ha - ha!
Who's a - fraid of the big bad wolf,
big bad wolf, big bad wolf? Who's a - fraid of the
big bad wolf? Tra la la la la.
Who's a - fraid of the big bad wolf, big bad wolf,
big bad wolf? Who's a - fraid of the big bad wolf?
1.
2.
G7
Tra la la la la. Came the la.

You've Got a Friend in Me

from Walt Disney's TOY STORY
Music and Lyrics by Randy Newman

Bridge
F
B
Now, some oth - er folks might be a lit - tle bit smart - er than I am,
C
B
big - ger and strong - er, too. May - be. But none of them will
Ddim7
Em
A7
Dm
G7
ev - er love you the way I do, just me and you, boy.
C
G7♯5
C7
F
F♯dim7
C
And as the years go by, our friend - ship will nev - er die.
Outro
F
F♯dim7
C
E7
Am
D7
G7
You're gon - na see it's our des - ti - ny. You've got a friend in me.
C
A7
D7
G7
C
G7
C
You've got a friend in me.

Zip-A-Dee-Doo-Dah

from Walt Disney's SONG OF THE SOUTH
Words by Ray Gilbert
Music by Allie Wrubel

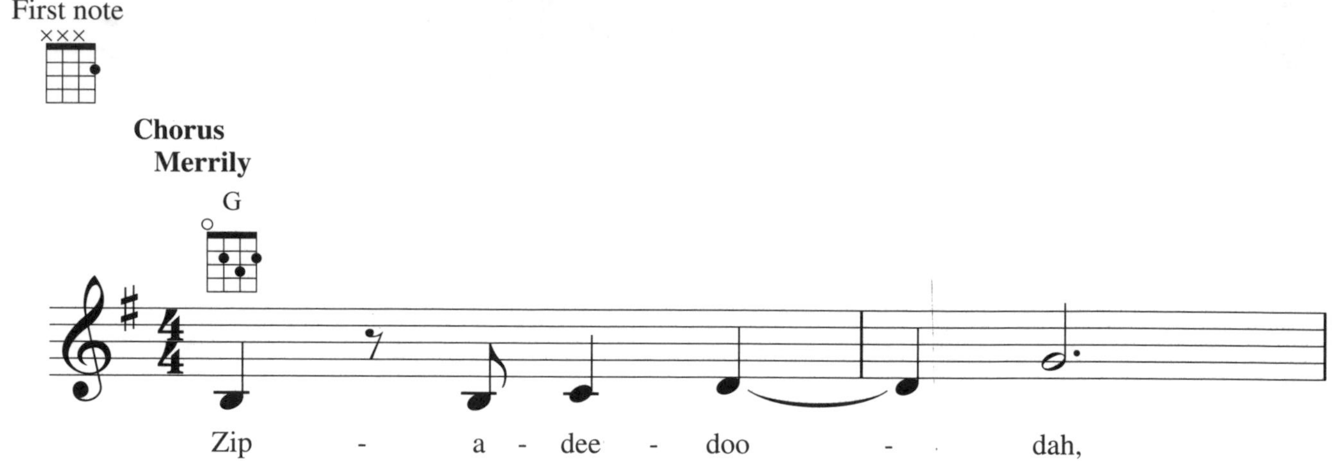

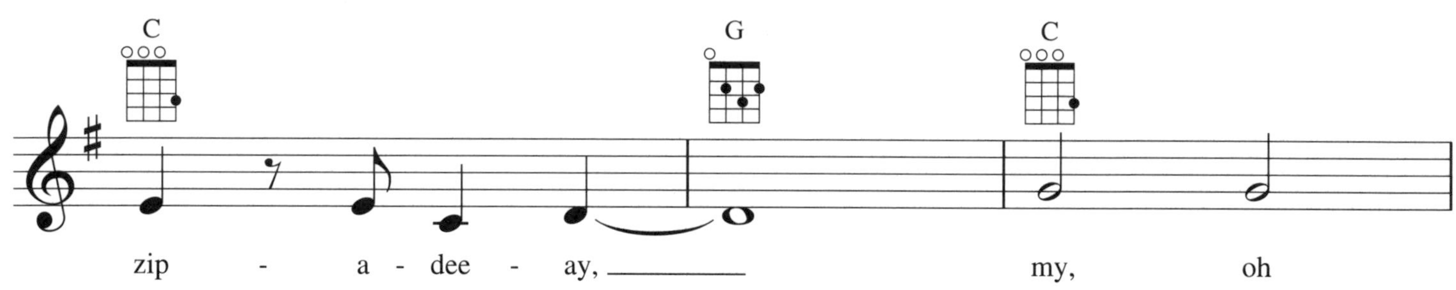

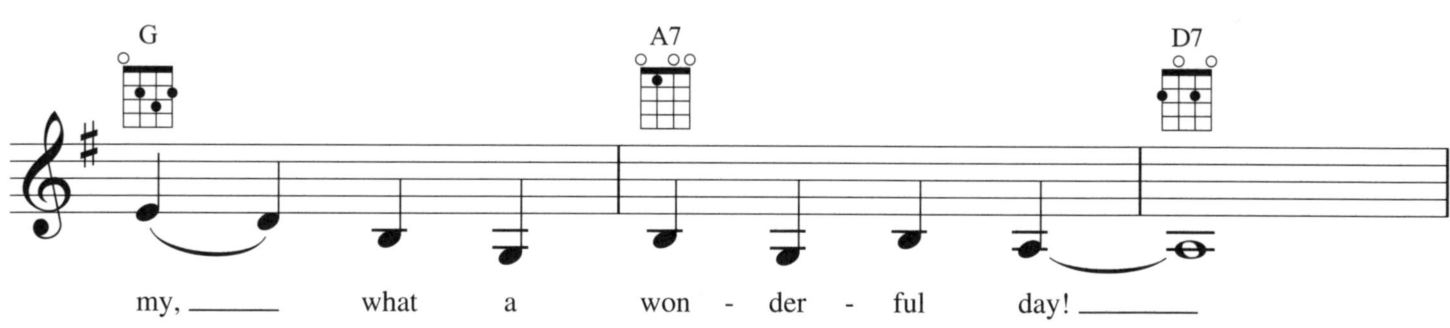

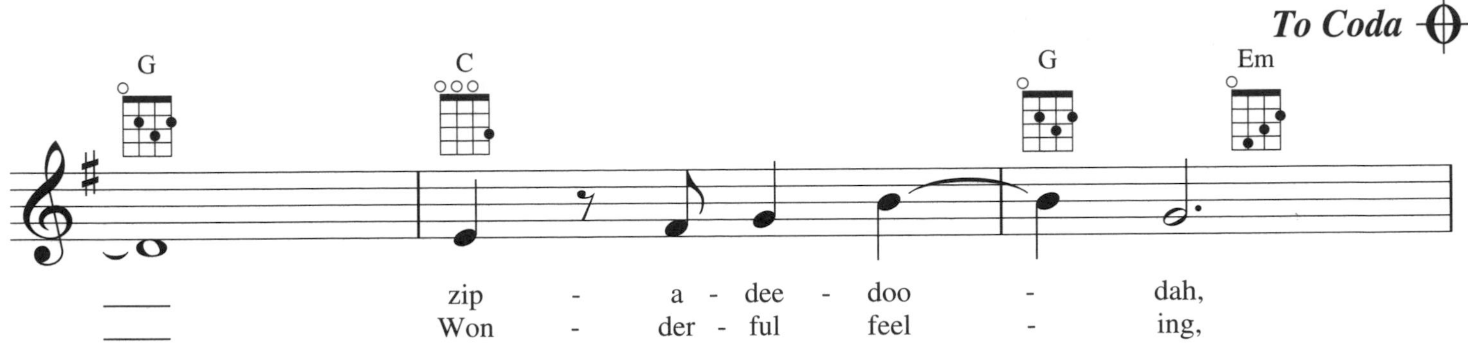
To Coda
G
C
G
Em
zip - a - dee - doo - dah,
Won - der - ful feel - ing,

Verse
Am
D7
G
D7
zip - a - dee - ay!
Mis - ter Blue - bird

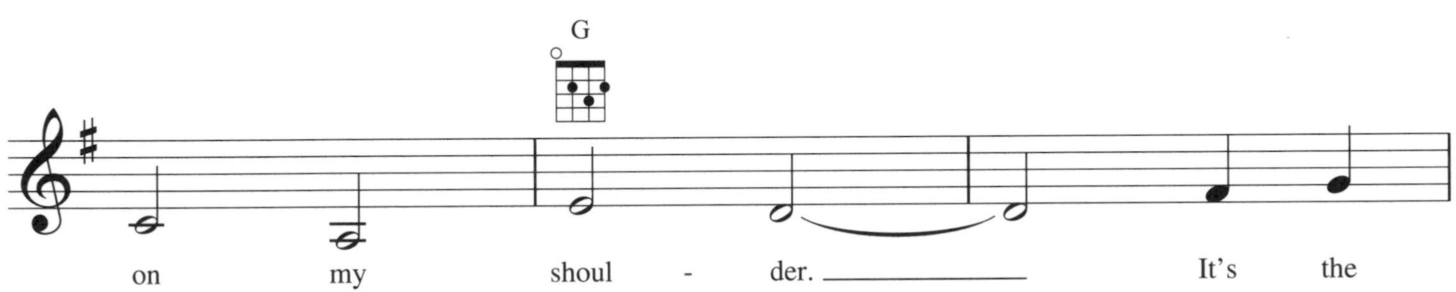
G
on my shoul - der. It's the

A7
D7
N.C.
truth, it's "act - ch'll," ev - 'ry - thing is

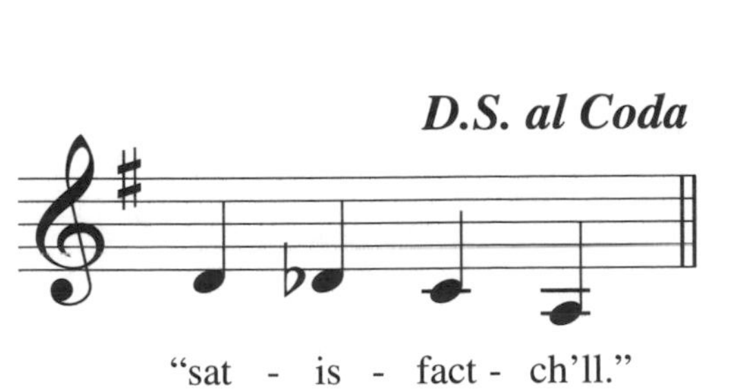
D.S. al Coda
"sat - is - fact - ch'll."

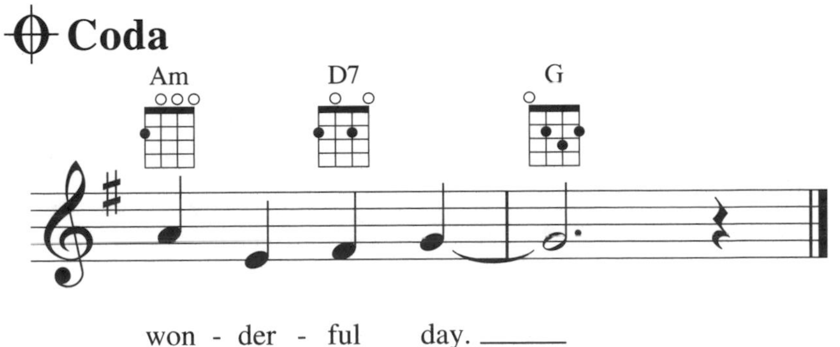
Coda
Am
D7
G
won - der - ful day.

We're All in This Together

from the Disney Channel Original Movie HIGH SCHOOL MUSICAL
Words and Music by Matthew Gerrard and Robbie Nevil

Pre-Chorus
F
E♭
F
Female: Ev-'ry - one __ is spe-cial in their own way; we make each oth - er strong. __
E♭
F
E♭
__ We're not the same; __ we're dif - f'rent in a good way.
Chorus
F
E♭
F
G
D
To-geth-er's where we be - long. __ All: We're all in this __ to-geth -
Em
G
C
G
C
D
- er; once __ we know __ that we are, __ we're all stars, __ and we see __ that. We're
G
D
Em
G
C
G
all in this __ to-geth - er, and __ it shows __ when we stand __ hand in hand, __
C
D
Fsus2
D.C. al Coda
(take repeat)
__ make our dreams __ come __ true. __ Ev-'ry - bod - y now:

Coda
Pre-Chorus
F Eb F
Female: We've ar - rived _ be - cause we stuck to - geth - er, cham - pi - ons one and all. _
Eb F
_ All: We're
Chorus
G D Em G
all in this _ to - geth - er; once _ we know _
all in this _ to - geth - er, when _ we reach, _
C G C D G D
_ that we are, _ we're all stars, _ and we see _ that. We're all in this _ to - geth -
_ we can fly, _ know in - side _ we can make _ it. We're all in this _ to - geth -
Em G C G
1.
C D
- er, and _ it shows _ when we stand _ hand in hand, _ make our dreams _ come... We're
- er; once _ we see _ there's a chance _ that we have _
2.
C D
_ and we take _ it.
Outro
G7sus4
Wild - cats ev - 'ry - where, wave your hands up in the air.
G
That's the way we do it; let's get to it, c' - mon, _ ev - 'ry - one! _